# Psychological Consequences of Terrorism

**ARTHUR T. POMPONIO, PH.D.**

**JOHN WILEY & SONS, INC**

SENIOR ACQUISITIONS EDITOR    Timothy Vertovec
ASSOCIATE PRODUCTION MANAGER  Kelly Tavares

This book was set in Times New Roman and printed and bound by Malloy Lithographers. The cover was printed by Phoenix Press.



ISBN 0-471-22815-X

Printed in the United States of America

10 9 8 7 6 5 4 3 2 1

# **CONTENTS**

# PSYCHOLOGICAL CONSEQUENCES OF TERRORISM

## RECALLING A DAY OF TERROR

On September 11, 2001 Mary S. was sipping her morning coffee at her kitchen window in an apartment in lower Manhattan. It was a few minutes before nine, and she was planning how her day would go—what she needed to prepare for work, the tasks waiting for her at her job, and how she would relax when she returned home. As she gazed calmly out her window, she noticed a flash of light as the first jetliner crashed into the north tower of the World Trade Center. In one horrific instant, everything changed. Mary sat transfixed as smoke started to billow from the building. Suddenly she felt a strong urge to be down below on the street. As she stared at the horror, she heard the second crash. From her location, she could see people running and crying and even more billows of smoke and fire. After a few stunned moments, she ran back into her apartment. From there, a little while later, she saw the first great tower collapse, then the second. As she later reported to the support group: "I saw all of it: the crashes, the falling buildings, the people running for their lives." She spoke movingly of how alone she felt in her pain and that she couldn't imagine how the pain would ever ease.

Jim B. listened quietly as Mary spoke about the terrible events. When it was his turn to discuss his own reactions to the attack, he described how moved he was by a collection of pictures drawn by school children that were posted on a building near where he lived. Some showed the intact towers standing tall. Others, he said, had written simple expressions of hope and love. Still others were just "sweet images of flowers and sunshine." Jim said the pictures gave him hope, "As terrible as the violence was, and as much as I know that our world had changed forever, those drawings really made me feel better. I knew we'd be OK."

Mary interrupted angrily, "Did you actually see the disaster?"

"No, I didn't. I live uptown. But I did see everything on TV. It was terrible."

Mary replied, now quite agitated: "No one who didn't directly see what I have seen—in real life—can possibly understand how horrible it all is. People who watched this on TV couldn't possibly get it. I don't want to hear about the future or happy pictures. I want to keep what I saw within me. I am not ready to 'get better.' You fool yourself if you think we'll be OK."

Greg remained silent throughout much of the support meeting. The therapist noticed that he seemed anxious and withdrawn. When the therapist asked if he had anything that he would like to say, at first Greg could say only one word: "anthrax." He began to tremble. After a few moments, he started to speak about his fear of bioterrorism, and how easy it would be for a terrorist to release anthrax into a dense urban population and wreak all sorts of havoc. His biggest fear of anthrax was that you could be "exposed to it without even knowing it, and then, if you couldn't be treated quickly enough you would die." The therapist encouraged Greg to speak about his fears, but also added some helpful information that addressed how he and the others in the group might address their fears in the long term. Greg felt some relief in knowing that there were steps he could take to help himself.

How did you respond to the horrors of September 11, 2001? For most Americans, this day may have changed their lives forever. For the first time in recent American history, most U.S. citizens experienced what many in the rest of the world have already endured: an extraordinarily violent act of terrorism. Whether in Kosovo, Jerusalem, Tokyo, Oklahoma City, or now New York City, people now know what it's like to be a victim of terrorism. Terrorism is the systematic use of intense fear by certain individuals, called *terrorists*, who intend to intimidate a population into meeting their demands. Terrorist acts often feel unprovoked and random. People experience a violent event and wonder: "Will it happen again?" "If so, when?" "What should I do to protect myself and those I care for?"

Acts of terrorism affect nearly everyone in the targeted population. Mental health practitioners assume that during such an intensely stressful period, everyone has been traumatized to some extent. Some appear immediately and profoundly affected, whereas others seem outwardly composed in the beginning and their reactions and symptoms only surface weeks or months later. Still others may never overtly demonstrate the effects that terror has had on them. The therapist facilitating the group noticed a defiant quality to Mary's talk, as though to *protect* her reactions to the experience, to keep them close. He understood Mary's need. Although he hoped that this protectiveness would in time lead to other feelings and coping mechanisms, for the time being Mary seemed to know what she needed to do to take care of herself. The therapist also understood Jim and Greg's very different reactions. At the moment, Jim was unwilling (or unable) to experience such intense feelings of fear and anger, and Greg needed help dealing with the new, unsettling fears of anthrax.

I am a psychotherapist in private practice in New York City. Mary, Jim, and Greg (not their real names) are clients from support groups I facilitated in the weeks following the September 11th attack. In counseling victims of terror, therapists and other mental health practitioners recognize the wide variety of possible reactions, and adapt their techniques accordingly. In this pamphlet, I plan to provide a brief overview of the immediate and long-term reactions to terrorism, followed by a summary of suggested methods for coping with this national tragedy. This pamphlet can never replace the work and benefits of actual therapy. It is designed as a brief, educational tool that may increase understanding of your own reaction to the crisis and that of your family, friends, and fellow Americans. It is also my hope that you will find useful tips for improving your coping skills and appreciation for reactions that may require further, professional help.

## REACTIONS TO TERRORISM: IMMEDIATE AND LONG-TERM

As we've seen with Mary, Jim, and Greg, terror can be experienced in a variety of ways. Each individual experiences a unique combination of physical, behavioral, and psychological reactions (see Table 1). In this section, we will examine both the immediate, common reactions, as well as, the long-term (or more extreme) reactions to terrorism. Before we begin, it is important to realize that *stress* is a core element of all our reactions. Therefore, it is necessary to first review what psychologists know about stress.

TABLE 1: Physical, Behavioral and Psychological Reactions to Stress

| Physical | Behavioral | Psychological |
|---|---|---|
| Heart palpitations | Unexpected gain/loss of weight | Depression |
| Dizziness | Unusual eating habits | Irritability |
| Trembling | Grinding of teeth | Anxiety |
| Headaches | Increased smoking | Withdrawal from the company of others |
| Perspiration | Increased alcohol or drug consumption | Difficulty in focusing on tasks |

TABLE 1: Physical, Behavioral and Psychological Reactions to Stress  *(continued)*

| Physical | Behavioral | Psychological |
|---|---|---|
| Dry throat | Sleep disturbances | Boredom |
| Aching or tense muscles (especially the back and neck) | Sudden crying | |
| Difficulty breathing | Nail biting | |

## What Is "Stress?"

Although it may seem strange, stress is not necessarily a bad thing. Physiologist Hans Selye defined **stress** as a "nonspecific response of the body to any demand made on it (Huffman, 2002, p. 96)." Whether you are in the middle of an exciting sports competition or trying to get to your job on time, certain physical, behavioral, and psychological results occur. Your heart may begin to race, you may start to bite your nails, and you may feel irritated. The trigger that prompts the stressful reaction is called a **stressor.** As you can see, a stressor can be either pleasant or unpleasant. Psychologists distinguish between beneficial stress, which they term **eustress** and deleterious stress, which they call **distress** (Huffman, 2002). Following common practice, however, in this document, we will use the term "stress" to refer to unpleasant or harmful stress.

Stress can result from such minor situations as hunting for misplaced keys when you are in a hurry to leave home to a catastrophic terrorist attack. The major sources of stress, however, include significant life change (death of a loved one, divorce, or a new job); chronic stressors, hassles, burnout, frustration, and conflict (Huffman, 2002). Of particular importance to understanding the psychology of terror are chronic stressors. **Chronic stressors** are those stressful situations that occur over time. Under normal circumstances, these might include a bad marriage, an unpleasant work situation, prolonged illness, and so forth. After September 11th, most Americans would have to add several new, previously unfamiliar chronic stressors, such as:

1. The uncertainty of knowing if or when a dangerous situation, such as a bombing or the release of lethal bacteria into the atmosphere, will occur
2. Having a common cold or flu, and fearing that you may have been infected by a deadly germ
3. Knowing that the nation is at war and that U.S. service personnel are in physical danger. (The impact of this chronic stressor is greatly intensified if you, or someone close, serves in the armed forces.)
4. The daily barrage of news describing the on-going, daily dangers of this war on terror

---

*Active Learning Activity*

In the space below, identify the chronic stressors you typically face during your average day. Then, make a separate list of those you have experienced since the September 11, 2001 terrorist attack and subsequent events.

---

To further appreciate the impact of terrorism, keep in mind that researchers have shown that stress in one area of our life can cause or increase stress in many others. Similarly, the stress we experience generally spills over onto the people we interact with, while their stress increases our own.

Now that we've reviewed the basics of stress, let's look at the variety of responses people commonly experience in the immediate, first few days and weeks following a terrorist attack.

## Immediate Reactions to Terrorism

Think back to a time when you experienced an immediate and intense physical sensation while facing a dangerous situation. To deal effectively with the immediate, direct danger, the sympathetic part of your autonomous nervous system sprang into action. It increased your heart rate, blood pressure, respiration, and muscle tension, while also decreasing the movement of stomach muscles, constricting your blood vessels, and releasing the hormones epinephrine and cortisol. These hormones activated your body to release stored fats and glucose into the bloodstream for an immediate increase of energy. This additional energy may have been used either to forcefully address the dangerous situation or to quickly escape from it (the so-called instincts of *fight* or *flight*, respectively).

Medical researchers and practitioners have identified other physical symptoms that can accompany extreme stress. These include headaches, nausea, and chest pain or palpitations and may require medical attention. Other physical symptoms include increased sense of fatigue or hyperactivity ("nervous energy"). Some people will experience pains in the neck or back. Other will have dizzy spells. Often, pre-existing medical conditions may worsen due to the stress.

In addition to physical and behavioral reactions, people also display various psychological reactions to terrorism. One common, immediate reaction to the overwhelming intensity of a terrorist act can be sudden and profound sense of shock to your usual emotional state. People might then feel dazed or stunned. Very often people cope with the threat of anxiety via defense mechanisms. **Defense mechanisms** are unconscious strategies to protect the mind (in psychoanalytic terms, a part of the mind called the ego) to reduce anxiety by distorting reality. There are many defense mechanisms that the mind employs to manage anxiety. Of particular importance to dealing with terror is denial.

**Denial** is the defense mechanism by which a person doesn't acknowledge that something very stressful has happened. It's as though in its attempt to protect itself from overwhelming anxiety, the mind tells itself "Nothing is wrong. Everything is fine." Could Jim B's reaction to the children's drawings possibly be an expression of denial? One important thing to remember about denial is that while it might not be in a person's best interest to maintain an unrealistic view about a painful truth, it might be necessary for some people to deny it for a time to keep from being overwhelmed by anxiety. When a person is in denial, he or she might not feel the full intensity of the event and may feel numb or disconnected from life.

Other defense mechanisms include *projection* (believing "All Muslims are dangerous terrorists," whereby one's own anger is projected onto an entire group of people), *idealization* (as in "All will be well because the President says so."), *rationalization* (believing "The U.S. brought the current terrorist environment entirely upon itself because of its failed foreign policy"). Note the quality of fantasy associated with each defense mechanism. The fantasy helps alter one's perception of a threatening reality. Notice too that even though these strategies are unconscious, very often we become aware of them in time.

Times of stress might also lead to strains in a person's relationships with others including family members, friends, coworkers, and classmates. This strain might be experienced by increased sense of annoyance. A person might notice that she or he is arguing more often that usual with others. A contrasting reaction might be for a person to withdraw from usual relationships as though to say, "I don't need anyone to help me get through this," or "I don't want anyone to see me so upset." Mary S. might feel like withdrawing from relationships when she says that she alone knows how terrible the events in New York City were and that no one could possibly understand how she feels.

---

*Active Learning Activity*

Psychological reactions to traumatic events are as varied and diverse as the people who experience them. In the following list of symptoms, place a check mark next to those you experienced in reaction to the recent terrorist activities.

- ❑  A sense of helplessness
- ❑  Feeling a loss of control
- ❑  Fearfulness
- ❑  A sense of vulnerability
- ❑  Grief
- ❑  Feelings of loss
- ❑  Xenophobia  (increased sense of distrust towards people from backgrounds than your own)
- ❑  Paranoia
- ❑  Recurring thoughts about the traumatic incident
- ❑  Interruptions of your usual behavior
- ❑  Survivor guilt ("Why did I survive when so many other people either were hurt or died?")
- ❑  Anxiety

How many of these feelings have you had? Are you able to talk about your feelings with anyone?

---

## Long-Term (or More Extreme) Reactions to Terrorism

Although anxiety and fear are common reactions to terrorism, some people develop lasting, extreme responses that significantly interfere with everyday functioning. These are known as **anxiety disorders**. **Anxiety** is an unpleasant emotional state of fear and apprehension (Davison & Neal, 2001). It occurs both in normal people and in those with certain forms of psychopathology. Although there is some evidence of genetic influence on the development of anxiety, the disorder is most likely due to stressful life circumstances. Stressful events experienced early in life contribute to anxiety disorders in adulthood (Westen, 2002).

*Anxiety disorders* are diagnosed when a person subjectively experiences anxiety that is particularly intense and sustained over time. The *Diagnosis and Statistics Manual*, Fourth Edition (DSM-IV), the document used by psychiatrists and psychologists to diagnose psychopathology, identifies six categories of anxiety disorder: phobias, panic disorders, generalized anxiety disorder, obsessive-compulsive disorder, post traumatic stress disorder, and acute stress disorder. Often a person who meets the diagnostic conditions of one disorder also meet those of another. This combination is referred to as **comorbidity**.

Although the trauma of living in a world of terrorism can lead to any one of several anxiety disorders— or worsen pre-existing ones—two are of particular concern: **acute stress disorder** and **post traumatic stress disorder**. They are similar in many ways; the principle difference between them relates to time. Symptoms associated with acute stress disorder first occur within four weeks of a traumatic event and last for at least two days. By contrast, post traumatic stress disorder lasts for more than four weeks.

According to the *Facts for Health* Web site, one in two people will be exposed to a life-threatening, traumatic event in their lifetime. However, while many people experience traumatic events, not everyone develops acute stress disorder or PTSD. On average, the organization notes, "10% of Americans have had or will have PTSD at some point in their lives, and that about 5% have PTSD at any given time." They also relate that women are twice as likely as men to develop PTSD. Both acute stress disorder and PTSD are outlined in detail in the DSM-IV-TR. Let's take a closer look at PTSD to get a clearer sense about anxiety disorders and how people experience them. The following list summarizes the main symptoms of the disorder. The complete diagnosis for both acute stress disorder and PTSD are presented in the Appendix.

***Post Traumatic Stress Syndrome (PTSD)***
1.  Re-experiencing the event through vivid memories or flashes
2.  Feeling "emotionally numb"
3.  Feeling overwhelmed by what would normally be considered everyday situations and diminished interest in performing normal tasks or pursuing usual interests
4.  Crying uncontrollably
5.  Isolating oneself from family and friends and avoiding social situations
6.  Relying increasingly on alcohol or drugs to get through the day
7.  Feeling extremely moody, irritable, angry, suspicious or frightened
8.  Having difficulty falling or staying asleep, sleeping too much and experiencing nightmares
9.  Feeling guilty about surviving the event or being unable to solve the problem, change the event or prevent the disaster
10. Feeling fears and sense of doom about the future

(*Source*: The American Counseling Association)

There are four types of PTSD:

1.  *Acute stress disorder* begins within four weeks of the traumatic event and lasts at least two days.
2.  *Acute PTSD* diagnosed if these same symptoms continue for more than four weeks
3.  *Delayed onset* PTSD is indicated if symptoms occur after four weeks from the time of the traumatic event
4.  *Chronic PTDS* becomes the diagnosis if symptoms last longer than 90 days.

(Source: Facts for Life Web site)

The *Facts for Health* Web site also notes that traumas of great severity (such as the jetliner crashes into the World Trade Center Towers) and those that occur over time (such as experiencing prolonged combat) are more likely to cause PTSD than acute stress disorder. Also, traumas that occur as the result of people interacting (such as a terrorist attack, a mugging, or sexual assault) are more likely to cause the disorder than natural disasters such as earthquakes or hurricanes. Finally, research shows that the very young, the very old, and those with other anxiety disorders are more susceptible to PTSD than others. Other psychological problems tend to accompany PTSD. These include panic disorder, agoraphobia, obsessive-compulsive disorder, social anxiety disorder, phobias, depression, sleep disorders, and substance abuse.

## COPING WITH TERRORISM:  WHAT CAN WE DO?

So far, we have examined the immediate and long-term, extreme consequences of a terrorist attack. Unfortunately, terrorism is more than just one terrible event such as an attack. It involves a protracted sense of fear that something else might happen. In the present day, many citizens of the U.S. are worried about bioterrorism, for example, in which terrorists release germs into the population with the intention of infecting individuals to make them sick or to kill them. Other people are worried about the detonation of nuclear bombs in dense urban areas. Although terrorists do want to inflict physical damage, they also want to disrupt the targeted population's sense of safety. This is a fear that must be faced as a new kind of social reality.

There are many practical steps that the federal, state and local governments can take to help make the population safer. To make flying safer, for example, uniformed and plain clothed marshals can be placed on every flight. Cockpits can be secured so terrorists cannot gain access to the flight controls of a jetliner. Baggage can be more carefully checked for weapons. And so forth. Yet a curious paradox emerges when these safety measures are taken: The very steps we take to protect ourselves can themselves make us more anxious because we wouldn't need them if there weren't anything to worry about in the first place.

## Problem-Focused Forms of Coping

What can we do to cope with these feelings? In the earlier section we noted that people often use defense mechanisms, such as denial, to cope with the immediate shock following a horrible tragedy. Some psychologists refer to these strategies as **emotion-focused forms of coping**. In contrast to emotion-focused forms of coping, psychologist have identified **problem-focused forms of coping** that use problem-solving strategies to decrease or eliminate the source of stress. This approach includes "identifying the stressful problem, generating possible solutions, selecting the appropriate solution, and applying the solution to the problem—thus eliminating the stress" (Huffman, p.108). In this section we will focus our attention on specific, problem focused forms of coping. Before we begin, try the following exercise.

---

*Active Learning Activity*
In the space provided, write a few paragraphs describing your experiences with the recent hostile events. Focus on your feelings. Consider how they may have changed over time.

---

Let's take a closer look at your previous experiences and coping strategies. Think back to an adverse circumstance that left you feeling frightened or helpless. Can you remember how you felt? Do you feel differently now? Try to remember what you did that helped you overcome your fears in that situation. Can you try the same thing now? Did it involve talking with others?  Remember, in stressful situations it is generally best to talk to others about your fears. If you do not have anyone with whom to talk, or you just do not feel like talking to those with whom you are close, you can find groups—either at work, school, or church, temple, or mosque—where people will be glad to speak with you. See page 14 for a list of suggested organizations to contact.

In addition to talking to others, many therapists advocate maintaining your usual routines. Familiar habits and responses can comfort us and help reorient us in a world that seems chaotic and strange. They also help us think positively. Chances are that life will get better. But it is important to remain realistic. Under stressful circumstances, what might seem like positive thinking might actually be denial. Also be realistic about the time it takes to feel better. It could easily take a while to return to some sense of normalcy. Don't rush yourself.

To further regain your sense of control and safety, here are a few direct and practical steps as identified by the American Counseling Association and the American Psychological Association. (For more information, visit www.counseling.org and www.apa.org.)

1.  Make it your business to know what the government is doing to combat terrorism and restore security.

---

### Active Learning Activity
Read three newspapers or magazine articles about steps the government has taken to restore personal safety and national security. In the space below, list five steps that have been taken. After each, write your reaction to the step taken. Is it helpful? What else could be done?

---

2.  Terrorism is designed to disrupt people's sense of control. To maintain (or regain) your sense of control, go about your daily business, while emphasizing those tasks and activities in which you excel. In this way you can help yourself to regain a sense of control. (It also helps to recognize—but not to dwell on—things that are outside of your control.)

---

### Active Learning Activity
List the things you enjoy doing or that you do well. Make an appointment with yourself over the next week to do at least two of these.

---

3.  Reduce stress by exercising your body. Exercise regularly within your ability.
4.  Participate in activities that engage your mind. Do a crossword puzzle; read a book; or do some gardening—whatever you find interesting to do.
5.  Humor can help. Read a funny book or watch a humorous television program.
6.  Individuals faced with other emotionally challenging situations, such as serious health problems or family-related difficulties, may have more intense reactions to the new stressful event and need more time to recover. Be sure not to lose sight of these earlier challenges. Keep appointments with doctors or psychotherapists.
7.  Eat nutritious meals and get plenty of rest.
8.  Avoid alcohol and drugs.
9.  Avoid major life decisions such as switching careers or jobs if possible because these activities tend to be highly stressful.
10. Limit your exposure to the news media. Anxiety can be heightened if you keep watching reports about terrorism.
11. Speak with those who care about you and who will listen and empathize with your situation. But keep in mind that your typical support system may be weakened if those who are close to you also have experienced or witnessed the trauma.
12. Seek professional help if you feel that your symptoms are worsening, persistent, or interfering with your daily functioning.

*Active Learning Activity*

Although the Appendix provides general contact information for national organizations that you can turn to for professional help, you can also find additional local support groups in the newspaper, telephone book, or your college counselors. List three organizations in your area that provide counseling or emotional support. Include addresses, phone numbers, and URLs. Even if you do not feel you need them for yourself, there may be someone in your life who could use the information.

1.

2.

3.

---

**THE AMERICAN COUNSELING ASSOCATION RECOMMENDS FIVE ADDITIONAL TIPS FOR COPING WITH CRISIS:**

1. Recognize your own feelings about the situation and talk to others about your fears. Know that these feelings are a normal response to an abnormal situation.
2. Be willing to listen to family and friends who have been affected and encourage them to seek counseling if necessary.
3. Be patient with people; fuses are short when dealing with crises and others may be feeling as much stress as you.
4. Recognize normal crisis reactions, such as sleep disturbances and nightmares, withdrawal, reverting to childhood behaviors and trouble focusing on work or school.
5. Take time with your children, spouse, life partner, friends, and co-workers to do something you enjoy.

*Source*: *American Counseling Association*

## Helping Children in Crisis

As adults we often find it difficult to understand and cope with trauma and stress. But most of us have resources to help: We have outside help, our cognitive capacities are more fully developed and we can better understand what is happening, and our emotional selves are more mature, and we can use previous emotional experiences to help us in the present. But what about children? They generally do not possess these resources. How can we help them manage the stress and anxiety associated with terrorism? The American Counseling Association provides the following suggestions.

- Encourage children to say how they are feeling about the event.
- Ask them to describe what they've seen, heard or experienced.
- Assure children that their parents are taking care of them and will continue to help them deal with anything that makes them feel afraid.
- Help them remember times when they've shown courage in meeting a new scary situation and accomplished a goal despite hardship or barriers. Instill a sense of empowerment.
- Let children know that institutions of democracy are still in place and our government is intact. (This reminder can also be helpful for adults.)
- Know that it is possible for children to experience vicariously personal traumatization from the terrorist attack (e.g. watching TV coverage, overhearing adult conversations).

Caretakers of children have an added responsibility to help young persons to cope. In doing so, they may also be helping themselves.

# COPING WITH THE UNTHINKABLE:  DEATH, BEREAVEMENT, AND GRIEF

In the fall of 2001, the United States finds itself at war against terrorism. Troops have been deployed to distant regions, the government is in a heightened state of emergency, and people are beginning to adjust and cope. However, there is one very profound source of stress that many of us will face that we have not discussed thus far: the death of a loved one.

War is by definition a sustained and violent act in which people die. As the horrific events unfold it is reasonable to assume that the number of people who have lost life will increase. We can help ourselves to face the death of others by examining what psychologists have learned about our responses to death, bereavement, and grief.

In times of personal loss, we most typically feel desolation, loneliness and heartache. In response, some people might cry, while others don't seem to feel anything at all. It is important to realize that people tend to react as they need to, that is within the context of their established defensive structures. Psychotherapists working with people who have lost loved ones try to help each person to find his or her way to best deal with death. It is also important to realize that specific reactions to loss might be powerfully influenced by social or cultural expectations. In our own culture, for example, many men have a hard time showing their emotions, particularly in public.

Although individuals react to death in their own ways, psychologists have identified what might be called a "normal" grieving process. This process involves four conditions: numbness, yearning, disorganization/despair, and resolution (James & Friendman, 1998; Parkes, 1972, 1991, cited in Huffman, 2002). The following outline specifies the emotional reactions associated with each condition.

1. *Numbness*. A person might feel stunned or a sense of emptiness. Some people might seem to feel very little. The defense mechanism of denial might be employed in an attempt to disavow a new and difficult reality.
2. *Yearning*. Here a bereaved person feels an intense longing for the deceased loved one along with feelings of guilt ("I should have insisted that my daughter not join the army."), anger ("Why did she have to join the army? It was stupid and selfish of her."), and resentment ("I hate life for taking her from me!"). Some people might even experience illusions such as believing that the man just "spotted" in a crowd is a deceased father.
3. *Disorganization/despair*. This phase generally occurs after the powerful emotions in the previous phase ease. Now a person might lose interest in life, or think that life without the lost person has no meaning. But this is also the period when acceptance starts to develop. Memories of being with the deceased are no longer just painful. We start to recall happy times. We also start to accept the death intellectually. And finally, we start to realize that with the passing of a loved one our own identities change. A bereaved person begins to understand that while she might no longer be a wife she is now a single woman.
4. *Resolution or reorganization*. With this last phase a person accepts more fully the loss and the changed circumstances of life.

It is important to underscore that though psychologists have determined this basic model of grieving, the experience varies for each person. Remember, too, that you should not expect your own grief to follow a formula. Be as generous with yourself as you might be towards another grieving person.

---

*Active Learning Activity*
In the space below, write a few paragraphs about how you or someone you know faced the death of a loved one. Did you or the person you know go through the phases outlined above?

---

## RESOURCES FOR HELP

After reading this pamphlet, you might feel that you want to know more about how to cope with terrorism. Remember, it can really help you to speak to someone about your feelings. If you would like to talk with a professional, but don't know how to find one, check with your school's medical or mental health department. To learn more about the psychological consequences of terrorism, you can also check out the following Web sites.

- American Counseling Association at www.counseling.org. This Web site provides a wide range of information about counseling. A link on the homepage connects you with information about terrorism.
- American Psychological Association at www.apa.org. This Web site provides information on a wide varietyof psychology-related matters. Visit the organization's internet site on the http://www.apa.org/psychnet/coverage.html to learn more about the trauma associated with terrorism. The site at http://helping.apa.org/find.html can help you to find a therapist in your area.
- Facts for Health at www.factsforhealth.org. This site provides information about acute stress disorder and post traumatic stress disorder.
- International Critical Incident Stress Foundation, Inc. (ICISF) at www.icisf.org. This site provides information about the management of stress. It offers links to many other valuable resources.
- U.S. Department of Health and Human Services at http://www.hhs.gov/hottopics/healing/biological.html. This site provides information about anthrax and the federal government's response to bioterrorism.

## APPENDIX: DSM-IV-TR DIAGNOSES OF TWO STRESS DISORDERS

### Post Traumatic Stress Disorder

The patient has experienced or witnessed or was confronted with an unusually traumatic event that has both of these elements:

1. The event involved actual or threatened death or serious physical injury to the patient or to others
2. The patient felt intense fear, horror or helplessness*

The patient repeatedly relives the event in at least 1 of these ways:
- Intrusive, distressing recollections (thoughts, images)*
- Repeated, distressing dreams*
- Through flashbacks, hallucinations or illusions, acts or feels as if the event were recurring (includes experiences that occur when intoxicated or awakening)*
- Marked mental distress in reaction to internal or external cues that symbolize or resemble the event
- Physiological reactivity (such as rapid heart beat, elevated blood pressure) in response to these cues

The patient repeatedly avoids the trauma-related stimuli and has numbing of general responsiveness (absent before the traumatic event) as shown by 3 or more of:
- Tries to avoid thoughts, feelings, or conversations concerned with the event
- Tries to avoid activities, people, or places that recall the event
- Cannot recall an important feature of the event
- Marked loss of interest or participation in activities important to the patient
- Feels detached or isolated from other people
- Restriction in ability to love or feel other strong emotions
- Feels life will be brief or unfulfilled (lack of marriage, job, children)

At least 2 of the following symptoms of hyperarousal were not present before the traumatic event:
- Insomnia (initial or interval)
- Irritability
- Poor concentration
- Hypervigilance
- Increased startle response

The above symptoms have lasted longer than one month.

These symptoms cause clinically important distress or impair work, social or personal functioning.

Specify whether: Recurring emotional reactions are common. Anniversaries of the event, such as at one month or one year, as well as reminders such as aftershocks from earthquakes or the sounds of sirens, can trigger upsetting memories of the traumatic experience. These 'triggers' may be accompanied by fears that the stressful event will be repeated.

*Source*: *Diagnostic and Statistical Manual of Mental Disorders-IV-TR*

## Acute Stress Disorder

The patient has experienced or witnessed or was confronted with an unusually traumatic event that has both of these elements:
1. The event involved actual or threatened death or serious physical injury to the patient or to others
2. The patient felt intense fear, horror, or helplessness

Either during the event or just afterward, the patient experiences 3 or more of these symptoms of dissociation:
- Feels numbed or detached or is unresponsive emotionally
- Seems less aware of surroundings, as in a daze
- Derealization
- Depersonalization
- Amnesia for important aspects of the event

The patient repeatedly reexperiences the event in one or more of these ways:
- Recollections (dreams, flashbacks, illusions, images, thoughts)
- The sense of reliving the event
- Mental distress as a reaction to reminders of the event

The patient strongly avoids activities, conversations, feelings, people, places or thoughts reminiscent of the trauma. There are marked symptoms of anxiety or hyperarousal, such as hypervigilance, insomnia, irritability, poor concentration, restlessness or increased startle response. At least 1 of the following applies:
- The patient feels marked distress from the symptoms
- They interfere with usual social, job or personal functioning
- They block the patient from doing something important such as getting legal or medical help or telling family or other supporters about the experience

The symptoms begin within 4 weeks of the trauma and last from 2 days to 4 weeks. The symptoms are not directly caused by a general medical condition or by substance use, including medications and Drugs of abuse. They are not merely a worsening of another Axis I or Axis II disorder.

Brief Psychotic Disorder is ruled out.

*Source*: *Diagnostic and Statistical Manual of Mental Disorders-IV-TR*

## References

**Books**

American Psychiatric Association. Diagnostic and Statistical Manual of Mental Disorders-IV-TR (1994). Washington D.C.: American Psychiatric Association

Davison, G and J. Neale, *Abnormal Psychology*, Eighth Edition (2001). New York: John Wiley & Sons, Inc.

Huffman, K. *Psychology in Action*, Sixth Edition (2002). New York: John Wiley & Sons, Inc.

Westen, D. *Psychology*, Third Edition (2002). New York: John Wiley & Sons, Inc.

**Web sites**

American Counseling Association (ACA) at www.counseling.org

American Psychological Association (APA) at www.apa.org

Facts for Health at www.factsforhealth.org

International Critical Incident Stress Foundation, Inc. (ICISF) at www.icisf.org

## Further Readings

The following books contain information regarding PTSD and its treatment.

Brisbey, S and L. B. Bisbey, (1998). *Brief Therapy for Post-Traumatic Stress Disorder: Traumatic Incident and Related Techniques*. New York: John Wiley & Sons, Inc.

Joseph, S, R. Williams and W. Yule, (1997). *Understanding Post-Traumatic Stress: A Psychosocial Perpsective on PTSD and Treatment*. New York: John Wiley & Sons, Inc.

Van der Veer, G. *Counselling and Therapy with Refugees and Victims of Trauma: Psychological Problems of War, Torture and Repression*, Second Edition (1998). New York: John Wiley & Sons, Inc.